HUDDERSFIELD

IN THE

TRAMWAY ERA

BRIAN HINCHLIFFE

TURNTABLE PUBLICATIONS
SHEFFIELD

First Published 1978

© Turntable Publications 1978

ISBN 0 902844 47 4

PRINTED IN GREAT BRITAIN
by
Henry Boot Group Printing

INTRODUCTION

Huddersfield, southernmost of the Yorkshire textile towns and world famous as centre of the fine worsted trade, ranked fourth in size in the former West Riding. The decennial censuses tell us that from 1881 to 1941, which neatly encompassed the tramway era in Huddersfield, the population increased steadily from 82,000 to 129,000. The lower part of the town lies in the Colne Valley, and from the confluence of the Rivers Colne and Holme, Chapel Hill climbs to the plateau on which the town centre is built. From there the suburbs extend into the surrounding hills, Castle Hill, the highest point within the Borough boundary, standing some 900 ft above sea level, though the highest point reached by trams was Mount Outlane at 850 ft.

Huddersfield had the distinction of being the first municipality in England to construct and operate its own tramways. The first tracks, of 4ft 7¾in gauge, were laid in 1881, and trial runs by steam tram took place on the 1 in 12 gradient of Chapel Hill in 1882. The success of these tests led the Corporation to buy more trams and inaugurate a public service to Lockwood, via Chapel Hill, in 1883. Other lines were laid in the Borough, as well as one in the neighbouring Urban District of Linthwaite, and by 1900 the combined route-mileage was 29½. In 1885 an experimental service of horse trams to Moldgreen, using the more level part of the Almondbury route, was introduced, but it lasted only till 1888; see Photograph 3.

Although the steam trams provided a public service, their shortcomings were both manifest and manifold. The success of electric trams in the neighbouring towns of Leeds (1891), Bradford (1898) and Halifax (1898) persuaded the Huddersfield authorities to electrify. A generating station and tram depot were built at Longroyd Bridge, while the tracks were rebuilt and overhead electric wiring installed to Edgerton and Lindley, Outlane, Longwood, Crosland Moor, and Slaithwaite via Linthwaite Urban District. The 4ft 7¾in gauge was retained, wide enough to take a broad, stable tram up the wind-swept hills, but unfortunately of unique width locally, the only other examples being in the Glasgow and Portsmouth areas. This made inter-running with Leeds (4 ft 8½ in), Bradford (4 ft 0 in) and Halifax (3 ft 6 in) impossible; these breaks of gauge were a serious handicap to inter-urban transport in the West Riding throughout the tramway period.

1. **The Early Years.** Views of the early electric tramways are shown in Photographs 4 to 25, beginning with Edgerton, and working round the system geographically in a counter-clockwise direction. The inaugural routes, to Outlane and the Edgerton-Lindley circle, were opened on 14 February 1901, and the other three within a fortnight. Map 1 shows the position soon after that date. The "Existing Routes" are the six which were opened for electric trams during the fortnight commencing 14 February 1901. The "Proposed Routes" include those to Sheepridge, Bradley, Waterloo, Almondbury, Stile Common, Honley, and Beaumont Park, which were already in existence, but operated by steam haulage; with the exception of the section from Lockwood to Beaumont Park, which was abandoned, all were later converted to electric traction. The "Proposed Routes", several of which were never in fact authorised, also include most of the later

3

electrified routes, but not Dod-Lea, Elland, or Fartown to Rastrick. Brighouse was to be served by a line from Birchencliffe and even more ambitious were the rural extensions to Holme Bridge, New Mill, Kirkburton, and Mirfield, but none of these was ever built. The whole system had been electrified by 1902.

The first services were operated by twenty-five uncanopied, open-top, bogie trams, in a smart red and cream livery. Photograph 12 shows No. 9 as delivered; its design was derived not from a steam tram, but from a lengthened double-ended horse tram. The travelling public were critical of the open tops and a top cover was designed in 1902 and fitted to several cars, as in Photograph 15. More trams were needed from 1902 onwards; they were all built as four-wheel open-toppers, in various classes, numbered between 26 and 70.

2. The Middle Years. By 1914 all the routes shown in Map 3 had been completed, except Longwood to Dod-Lea (1920), and Fartown to Brighouse (1923). The latter was an important extension, ¾-mile of which, near Fixby, was on a sleepered private reservation; it brought the route mileage of the system to its maximum figure of 38¾. Meanwhile much of the track was rebuilt, some lengths of single line doubled and the whole network restored to sound operational condition. Map 2 shows the route layout in the central area at this time. John William Street, of which several pictures are included, is the northern continuation of New Street. King Street, Kirkgate and Viaduct Street were operated as one-way streets by the trams.

This period also saw the emergence of the standard Huddersfield tram, whose numbers finally ran from 71 to 126 (Photograph 30), and many of the older cars were given Bellamy-type top covers (Photograph 25) with seated open canopy and a neater appearance. About 1915 service numbers were introduced, displayed by a stencil, and later by blind.

3. The Final Years. In 1924 a totally-enclosed version of the standard car was purchased, ten being built, numbered 127 to 136 (Photograph 67), while most of the older cars were vestibuled (Photograph 55). In 1931 a more modern design appeared, having upholstered seats, more powerful motors and air-brakes; eight were built, numbered 137 to 144 (Photograph 63). These were still in good order when withdrawn in 1938, and were sold to Sunderland Corporation where, after re-gauging, they worked for a further sixteen years. These cars came too late to prolong the tramway era, for beginning in 1933 the system was converted in seven years to trolleybuses, which in their turn were replaced by diesel buses.

I am much indebted to the Chief Librarian of Kirklees Libraries for permission to use Photographs 1—3, whose original negatives are held by the Library; to the Local History Department of Kirklees Library for their assistance; to M. J. O'Connor for the loan of seven of the early photographs; and to W. A. Camwell for the use of Photographs 54, 56, 67 and 72; the remainder are from the collection of H. B. Priestley.

B. HINCHLIFFE.

1. This splendidly-evocative view of St. George's Square recaptures the whole atmosphere of late-Victorian provincial England, with its hansom cabs, horse drays, open carriage, and granite sets, liberally bestrewn with horse manure. The steam tram and trailer are working the Waterloo service, as can be seen from the destination boards on the side of the tram and on the front of the locomotive. Notice the condenser on the roof of the latter and the skirts almost to road level to prevent accidents in the wheels and motion. Even the headless woman in the foreground does not look out of place.

5

2.	This shot outside the Junction Hotel at Moldgreen is believed to be the only photograph in existence of a Huddersfield horse tram, whose existence spanned only the three years 1885—1888. Notice the bowler hatted, non-uniformed driver and conductor, also the trace boy.

3.	A busy scene in John William Street, seen from the lower end of St. George's Square. Three trams are facing south, the nearest one showing Almondbury on its destination board. In the distance a fourth tram is approaching. How splendidly young Victorian womanhood carried itself.

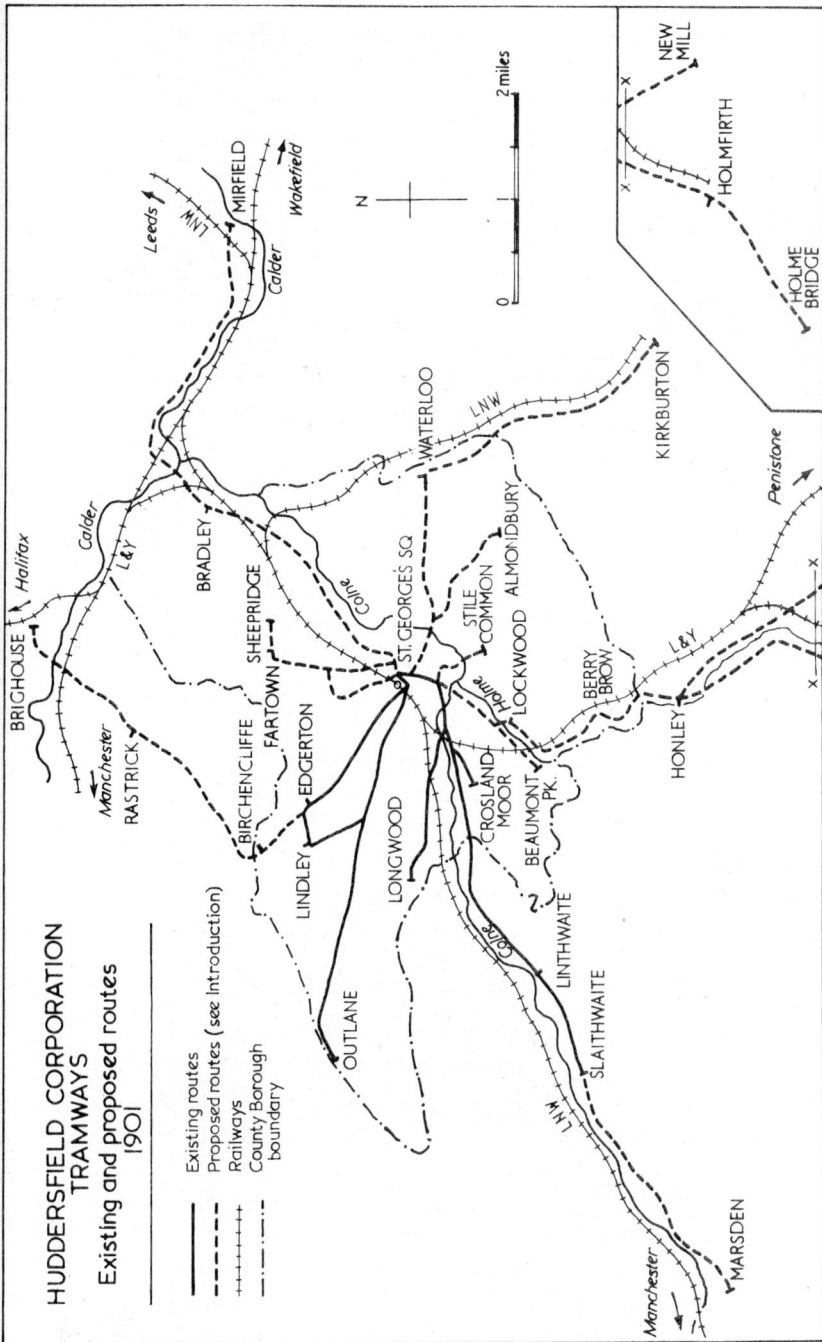

HUDDERSFIELD CORPORATION TRAMWAYS

Existing and proposed routes 1901

	Existing routes
	Proposed routes (see Introduction)
	Railways
	County Borough boundary

Map 1. Huddersfield Corporation Tramways in 1901.

NEW MILL
HOLMFIRTH
HOLME BRIDGE
KIRKBURTON
Penistone
WATERLOO
LNW
Leeds
MNT
MIRFIELD
Calder
Wakefield
N
2 miles
0
BRIGHOUSE
Halifax
Calder
L&Y
Manchester
RASTRICK
BRADLEY
SHEEPRIDGE
BIRCHENCLIFFE
FARTOWN
EDGERTON
LINDLEY
LONGWOOD
OUTLANE
St. GEORGE'S SQ.
Colne
STILE COMMON
ALMONDBURY
LOCKWOOD
BERRY BROW
HONLEY
L&Y
CROSLAND MOOR
BEAUMONT PK.
LINTHWAITE
SLAITHWAITE
Colne
MNT
MARSDEN
Manchester
Holme

7

4. Looking down New North Road towards Westgate. The overhead wires are supported by span wires because the road is too wide for side brackets. A car of batch 1—25 can be seen in the distance waiting at a passing loop, before coming up the hill to Edgerton.

5. **Looking up Holly Bank Road from Halifax Road at the beginning of the Edgerton-Lindley Circular route. The rural surroundings explain why the route was a commercial fiasco.**

6. **The top end of Holly Bank Road. Despite protests by local residents the circular route was abandoned on 14 October 1911.**

7. A view of Lindley Terminus taken about 1904. As the circular route was still open this was not strictly a terminus at the time; the track can be seen curving into Holly Bank Road in the foreground. Car No. 27, of Class 26—31, is standing opposite the passenger shelter in Lidgett Street. The roller blind reads "Edgerton Lindley". Notice the smartly uniformed staff.

8. On 6 June 1905 the brakes failed on car No. 67, causing it to leave the rails in spectacular fashion on the Edgerton Circular and plough through a wall on to private land. It is seen here being prepared for jacking up and re-railing.

9. A puzzle photograph. The background is an early commercial view of car No. 16 and two others in John William Street, looking north, but the foreground has been taken from another photograph and superimposed, introducing letterbox, lamp-post and pedestrians in place of tram tracks.

10. Another view looking north along John William Street from approximately the same standpoint, a short time later. Car No. 45 of Class 43—56, with early type of top covers can be seen in the distance and beyond that an open-topper with its trolley pole being reversed.

11. Looking north along New Street. Car No. 37 of Class 32—42, with balcony and reversed stairs, is turning into King Street. The blind shows "Moldgreen Waterloo". To judge by the gawping spectators photography was still a novelty. Notice the high telegraph poles above the roofs in the distance.

12. A further view of New Street looking north. Car No. 61, on its way to Lockwood approaches the camera. Notice the sandwich board advertisement, mounted on wheels and the number of boys wearing Eton collars.

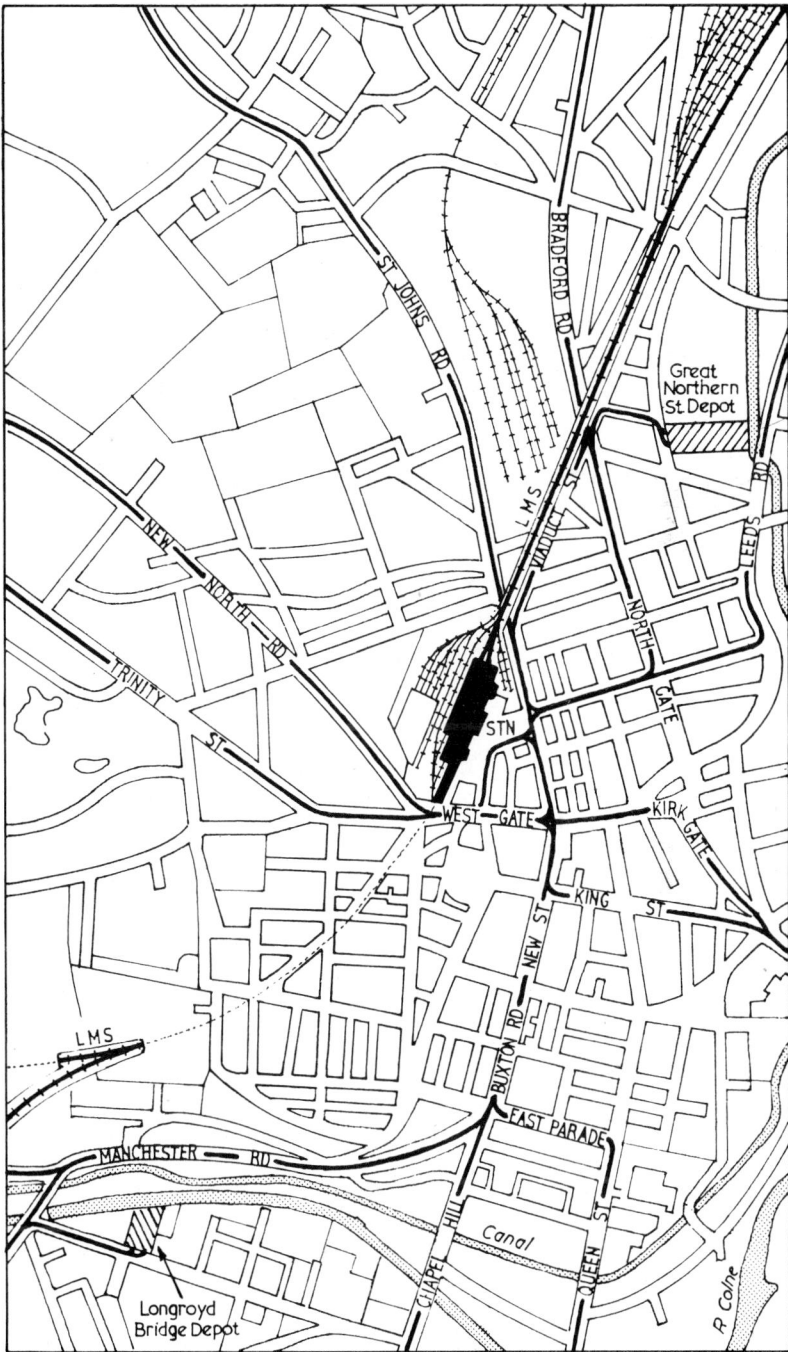

Map 2. The Central area at maximum extent.

13. A very early view of car No. 9 in original condition, bearing the legend "Huddersfield Corporation Electric Tramways" on the rocker panel and "Paddock and Longwood" on the board above. The driver and conductor are wearing the 1901 pattern uniform and cap, which are not dissimilar from those worn by the postman on the left.

14. Car No. 46 and crew pose for this shot in Manchester Road, en route to Slaithwaite, about 1902.

15. Car No. 21, with the early type of top cover, stands at Slaithwaite terminus, prior to making the return trip to Huddersfield.

16. Car No. 17 stands at the 1901 terminus at Crosland Moor. The standard pattern Corporation passenger shelter is partly obscured by the bevy of children in the garb of the period. The combination of cloth cap, Eton collar, breeches and clogs appears odd, especially when accompanied by a gold Albert and chain, on a small schoolboy.

17. On 3 March 1906 the brakes failed on car No. 26 and instead of negotiating the bend from Newsome Road into Colne Road it jumped the tracks and finished up against a house side, to the great interest of the youth of the neighbourhood.

18. Car No. 31 seen at Almondbury terminus in its original condition. Notice the mitred windows, externally-sprung trolley-pole and letterbox mounted on the outside front panel; the last was a well-known Huddersfield facility. Notice also the lengthy extract from the Bye-laws below the nearside bulk-head window.

19. Car No. 64, of Class 62—66, seen on the Almondbury service after acquiring a Milnes, Voss top cover. The space devoted to advertising on the tram appears exceptional even for those days.

20. Bogie tram No. 24 after leaving the track at Bradley.

21. A fine early photograph at Waterloo terminus. Car No. 34, showing "Moldgreen Waterloo", appears to be in the charge of the conductor, while the driver stands in the road, which is thick with mud. Note the rigid suspension of the overhead wires.

22. Another fine early photograph, this time of car No. 12 at Bradley terminus. Apart from the box destination indicator (compare Photograph No. 13) the tram is exactly as supplied. Notice the various headgear in evidence. In the middle distance can be seen the Lancashire & Yorkshire Railway main line and Cooper Bridge station.

23. Car No. 18 after the first major modifications, which included a wide-wing truck instead of the original bogies and an internally-sprung trolley pole. The side indicator shows "Market Place & Birkby".

24. The upper end of Westgate, looking east. The date must be prior to 1908, when the single line was doubled. The tracks leading to the station and St. George's Square can be seen turning off to the left.

25. The lower end of Westgate, taken about 1915. The flags suggest the celebration of an Allied victory. Car No. 29, with Bellamy-type top-cover, is on the Lindley via Oakes service. Note the conductor carrying the post-box round to attach to the rear bracket.

26. Fare Stage 15 at Burn Road corner, Birchencliffe, seen about 1920. Car No. 43, bearing Service No. 7, is en route to Elland.

27. Part of Elland, seen from Hullen Edge. A highly characteristic West Riding scene with its mills, terrace houses, river and steep hills. Car No. 41, from West Vale to Huddersfield, climbs the single track to Elland by the side of the high retaining wall.

28. Looking down Saddleworth Road to West Vale tram terminus, where an unidentified car is standing. Even the washing hanging out over the pavement cannot relieve the gloom of drab stone walls, stone roofs, stone pavements and stone sets over the full width of the road. Halifax Corporation's Stainland route crosses Saddleworth Road at right angles at the bottom of the dip.

29. Another view of West Vale terminus, looking up the hill towards Elland. Car No. 68, of Class 68—70, fitted with a Bellamy top-cover, awaits departure for Huddersfield.

HUDDERSFIELD CORPORATION
TRAMWAYS - 1930

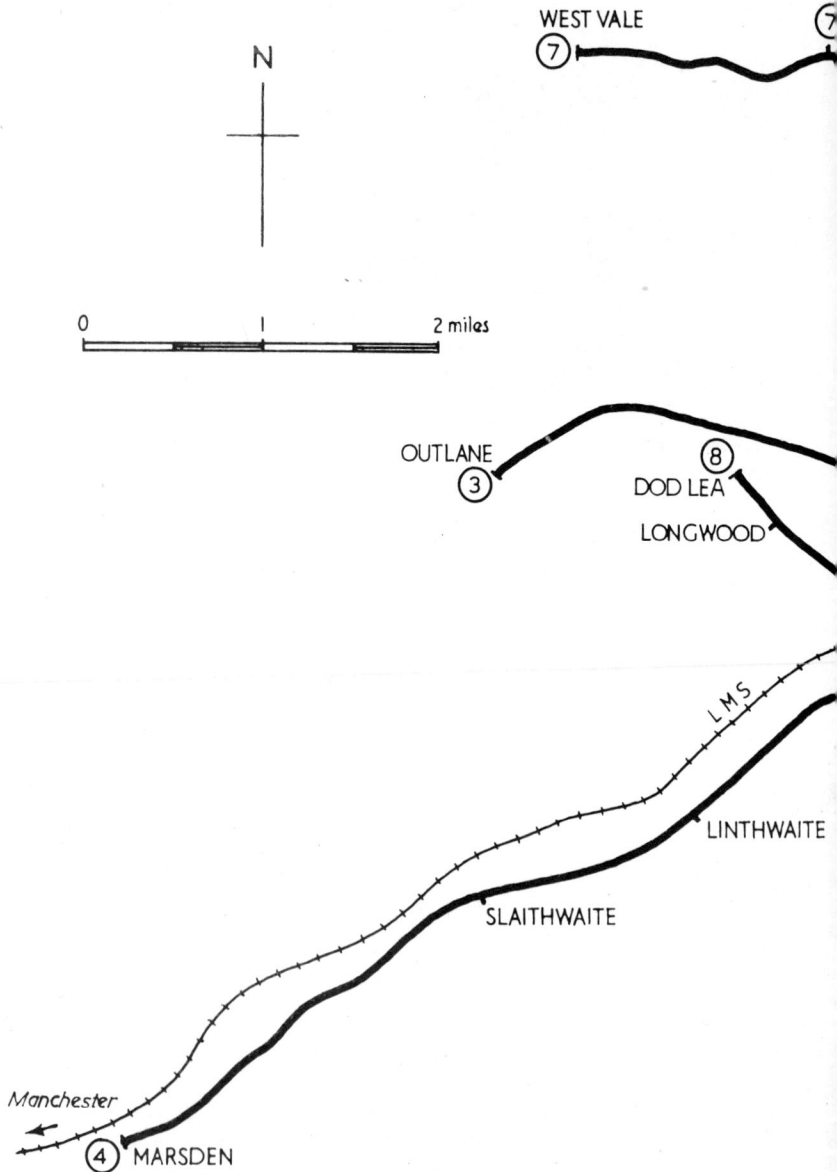

N

0   1   2 miles

WEST VALE
⑦

⑦

OUTLANE
③

⑧

DOD LEA

LONGWOOD

L M S

LINTHWAITE

SLAITHWAITE

Manchester

④ MARSDEN

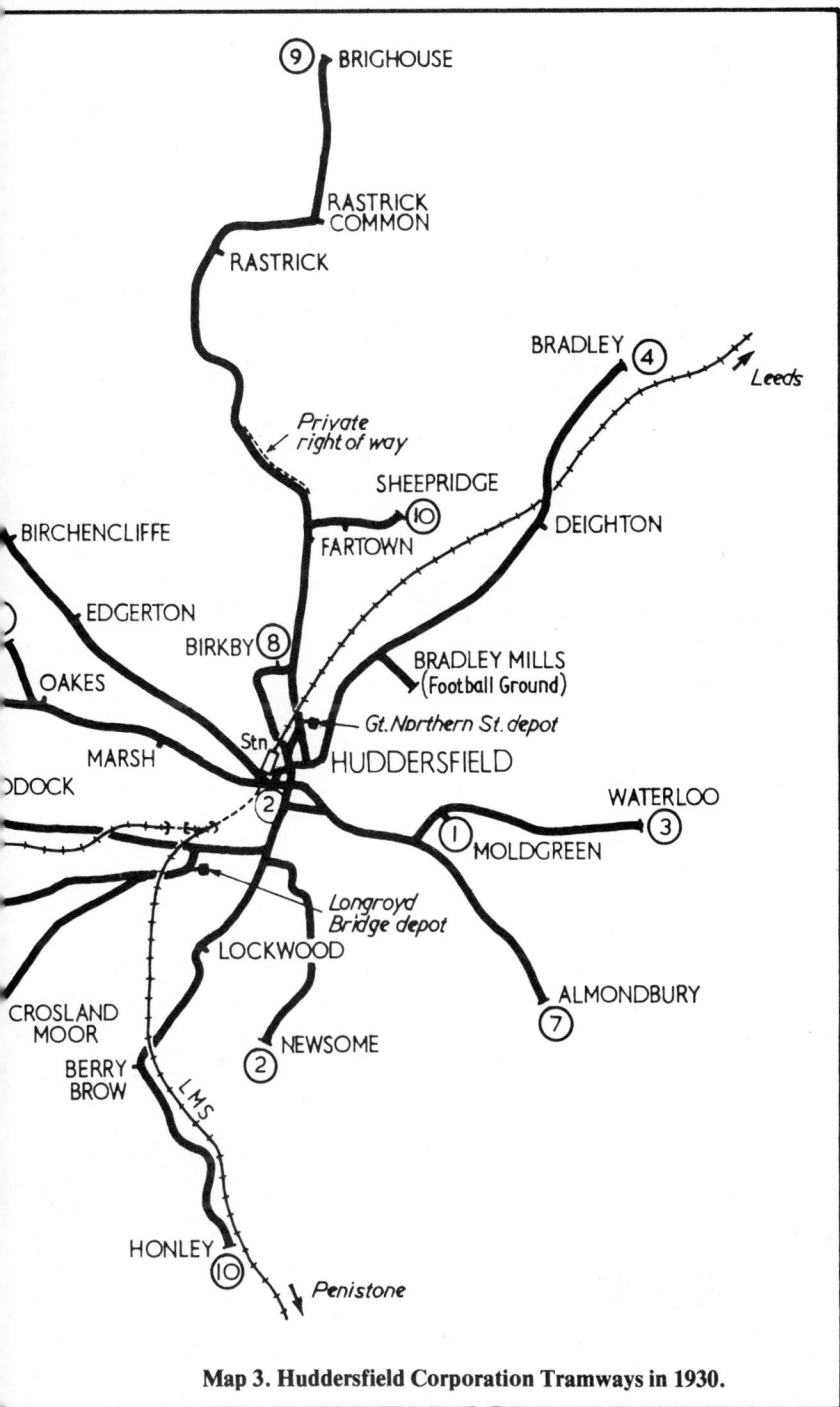

Map 3. Huddersfield Corporation Tramways in 1930.

BRIGHOUSE ⑨

RASTRICK COMMON

RASTRICK

Private right of way

SHEEPRIDGE ⑩

FARTOWN

BRADLEY ④

Leeds

BIRCHENCLIFFE

DEIGHTON

EDGERTON

BIRKBY ⑧

BRADLEY MILLS (Football Ground)

OAKES

Gt. Northern St. depot

Stn

MARSH

HUDDERSFIELD

ODDOCK

② WATERLOO ③

① MOLDGREEN

Longroyd Bridge depot

LOCKWOOD

ALMONDBURY ⑦

CROSLAND MOOR

② NEWSOME

BERRY BROW

LMS

HONLEY ⑩

Penistone

30. Looking west up Trinity Street towards Outlane, about 1926. Car No. 82 is of the Standard Class 77—126, built from 1912 onwards, with canopy top-covers and vestibuled platforms.

31. A further view of the same route, this time looking down Westbourne Road, towards the town centre.

32. Car No. 45 on the Moldgreen & Lindley service, near Lindley terminus, after the abandonment of the Edgerton Circular. Notice the rod for releasing the life-guard and the bracket for the post-box.

33. Looking west up New Hey Road, at Salendyne Nook. Standard Car No. 78 is climbing towards the terminus at Outlane.

34. Car No. 75, of Class 71—76, stands at Outlane terminus, the highest point reached by Huddersfield trams. The track and single wire leading off to the left enabled coal trams to reach Gosport Mills.

35. Looking north along John William Street from its junction with Westgate/Kirkgate, almost the same point as in Photograph 9. Notice the policemen about to exchange white coat and point duty.

36. Looking down New Street towards the point seen in the previous picture. Car No. 17 is showing "Cowlersley Lane" (a point on the Slaithwaite route) on its indicator. The flags suggest the photograph was taken during the First World War.

37. The triple junction at the top of Chapel Hill, looking north along Buxton Road, about 1924, taken from the top deck of a north-bound car. The car for Newsome, Service 2, is about to turn left into East Parade.

38. A close-up of the Buxton Road junction. Car No. 8 is on Service 8 and going into town from the Paddock direction, on its way to Birkby. The date is about 1928 and much of the commercial traffic is still horse-drawn.

39. A view at Longwood terminus before the line was extended to Dod-Lea. The date is before the First World War and although Stalin was reputed to be living in England at the time, it is quite certain he was not employed as a Huddersfield tram conductor despite the above photographic evidence.

40. In 1914 the Slaithwaite route was extended to Marsden which, with a length of 7¼ miles, became Huddersfield's longest route. Note how the bracket arms have lost the elaborate adornment of earlier years. Car No. 72 is about to leave while No. 96 awaits access to the single line section.

41. Car No. 44 is caught at Park Road West on the outward journey to Crosland Moor. The indicator reads "Crosland Moor for Beaumont Pk." The track curving towards the camera is a relic of the former reversing triangle for steam trams.

42. The final terminus of Service 6 at Crosland Moor, showing the trolley reverser. Car No. 54 is showing "St. George's Square" on the indicator; for many years this and the Newsome service were the only ones which did not operate across town.

43. The terminus at Newsome was typical of Huddersfield practice, with overhead trolley reverser, Corporation-type passenger shelter, etc.

44. An identical set-up existed at Honley, where car No. 124, complete with post-box, is about to return to the town.

45. King Street was operated as a one-way street for trams. The driver of car No. 62, for Almondbury, awaits the starting bell, some time about 1924.

46. Another view of the terminus at Waterloo, taken some twenty years later than Photograph 21. Apart from the road, which is now surfaced with sets, and the improved overhead wiring, there is little difference in the scene.

47. The middle years close with the appearance of buses. No. 7, with CX registration, is elaborately lined out and mounted on solid tyres, which gave a hard ride on the set-paved roads. Only the wheeled traffic shows much change in the quarter century since Photograph 1.

48. The final years open with a later view, taken in May 1937. Car No. 77, still with open balcony, shows "Football Special" on the rear indicator and "Huddersfield" on the side. The wiring for trolleybuses is already partially installed.

49. Looking up Westgate in the early 1930s. The track is now doubled and car No. 116 is making its way towards Lindley. The traffic is so sparse that the policeman on point duty seems an unnecessary luxury.

50. Another view of Westgate looking in the opposite direction. Car No. 84, coming up the hill, is on the way to Outlane.

51. The summit of the West Vale route was at Ainley's Top, some 700 ft above sea level. This view, looking down towards Elland and the Calder Valley, was taken in 1938 from the point where the Motorway now crosses over.

52. The sharp elbow curve known as Ainley's Bend is some quarter of a mile lower down the hill than the last photograph. One day in April 1939 No. 96's trolley-pole came off the wire and became entangled with the trolleybus wires. As the crew were unable to free it with the bamboo pole, the following car, No. 89, had to attach the tow-bar and draw No. 96 up the hill to free the trolley-pole.

53. Passengers from Huddersfield on car No. 84, bound for West Vale, alight in Elland in July 1936. The building in the right background, which was reputed to be a former prison, bears the legend "Elland Urban District Council Bus & Tram Passengers Shelter".

54. Car No. 89 leaves the centre of Elland for West Vale in January 1939. That week the Palladium was showing "Nothing Sacred" and "Romance and Rhythm".

55. Just beyond the point in the previous photograph, the tram route turned from Victoria Road into Jepson Lane. In August 1936 rush hour extras were still worked by the older trams, such as No. 63 seen here. The absence of rush hour road traffic is noticeable.

56. Compare this view of West Vale terminus, taken in April 1938, with the similar scene in Photograph 29.

57. Looking along Acre Street, Lindley, about 1930. The terminus can be seen in the distance.

58. The registration numbers suggest that this view of New Street, looking north, was taken about 1930. The woman driver in the nearest vehicle would certainly be a rarity at the time. Car No. 78, on its way from the depot to Moldgreen, is just passing an open charabanc labelled "Excel". At this time Huddersfield still had some two-digit telephone numbers.

59. Car No. 126 passes the Royal Oak at Church Street/Clough Lane corner on its way to Dod-Lea. The trolleybus wires have already been erected and the live wire is being used by the tram. June 1938.

60. Dod-Lea terminus in May 1937.

61. Car No. 116 enters the top passing loop on the Crosland Moor route, in May 1937.
The shot was taken from the balcony of an inward-bound car. Both were using the
recently-installed trolley wires.

62. **The Parkgate passing loop at Berry Brow, looking south towards Honley. Enclosed car No. 133 is seen running towards St. George's Square in June 1938.**

63. **Car No. 143 of the final Huddersfield design, standing at Honley terminus. Apart from the traffic lights, M.o.T. road numbers, telephone kiosk and disappearance of the tram shelter, little has changed since Photograph 44 was taken.**

64. Looking north across Colne Bridge, in Queen Street, on the last day of tram operation on the Newsome route, 1 May 1937. Car No. 54 running towards the town centre is passed on the wrong side by three private cars.

65. Looking through the L.M.S. viaduct towards Bradford Road, in June 1939. The junction on the left into Viaduct Street has already been disconnected, but the one on the right to Great Northern Street depot is still in use. By this time post-boxes were no longer being carried. At their maximum use, the G.P.O. cleared the boxes hourly, collecting all day on every tram and taking over 20,000 letters weekly. In later years buses and trolleybuses carried post-boxes on two trips each day.

66. Fartown junction, with the branch to Sheepridge diverging to the right. Cars Nos. 130 and 114, running to and from Brighouse respectively, are taking their current from the trolleybus wires already installed.

67. Car No. 135 seen at Sheepridge terminus in June 1938, a few days before trams were replaced by trolleybuses. Notice the Jowett car on the left.

68. At the New Inn, Netheroyd, the tram route to Brighouse diverged from the main road and entered the Fixby reserved track. Here car No. 123 is seen rejoining the main road in June 1939.

69. Cars Nos. 108 and 119 pass on the reserved track at Fixby. This view, looking north, was taken in 1936.

70. The top end of Fixby reserved track seen from Bradley Lane, Rastrick, in June, 1936. The trolley wheel actuates the signal on the left, which falls into the lower quadrant to give access to the single-line in the foreground.

71. Car No. 110 climbing southwards from Brighouse towards Rastrick in July 1938. The masts are already in position for trolleys, but the wires have not yet been slung.

72. Car No. 119 stands at Brighouse terminus in April 1938, prior to leaving on the cross-town route to Marsden (Sundays only), which was over 12 miles in length. The tracks of the former Halifax Corporation route have already been lifted and the road resurfaced, as can clearly be seen in the distance.

73. The siding at Bradley Mills, outside Huddersfield Town football ground, with cars Nos. 60, 43 and 68 waiting for the end of the match.